CONTENTS

Get out into space medley (handwritten)

Produced by STEPHEN CLARK and SADIE COOK
Cover artwork © Pola Jones Associates Ltd.
First Published 1993

Folio © International Music Publications Limited
Griffin House 161 Hammersmith Road London W6 8BS England

215-2-984

AIN'T GONNA WASH FOR A WEEK

Words by PETER UDELL
Music by GARY GELD

4

gon-na pro-tect that beau-ti-ful spot. You can call me "Kook-ie" But

nev-er-the-less, I ain't a-gon-na wash a-way a sin-gle ca-ress! You can

tell me "What's a lit-tle old kiss on the cheek" But I ain't a-gon-na wash for a

week, no, no! I ain't a-gonna wash for a week! week!

ALL SHOOK UP

Words and Music by
OTIS BLACKWELL and ELVIS PRESLEY

DON'T LET ME BE MISUNDERSTOOD

Words and Music by BENNIE BENJAMIN,
SOL MARCUS and GLORIA CALDWELL

Ba-by do you un-der-stand me now,_____ Some-times I feel a lit-tle mad, But don't you know that no-one-a-live can al - ways be an an-gel

When things go wrong I seem to be bad But I'm just a soul who's in-

-ten-tions are good Oh! Lord Please don't let me be mis-un-der-

-stood.

GLORIA

Words and Music by
VAN MORRISON

GOOD VIBRATIONS

Words and Music by
BRIAN WILSON and MIKE LOVE

Same

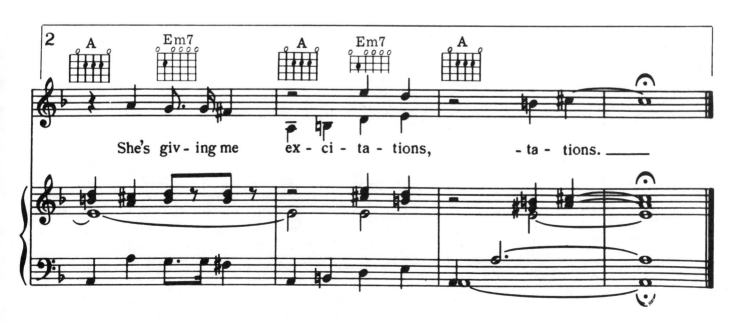

GO NOW

Words and Music by
LARRY BANKS and MILTON BENNETT

How man-y times_ do I have to tell you dar-lin', Dar-lin' I'm still in love _ with you now. _____

For Repeat We've al-read-y said _ *Last time*

I don't wan-na see you go,_ But dar-lin' you'd bet-ter GO NOW.

Additional Lyric So—long—
I don't want to see you go,
But you had better
Go now.
Go now, Go now,
Go now.
Don't you even try— to tell me
That you really want to see it end this way
'Cause darlin'— darlin'—
Can't you see— I want you to stay.

GREAT BALLS OF FIRE

Words and Music by
JACK HAMMER and OTIS BLACKWELL

I'M GONNA CHANGE THE WORLD

Words and Music by
ERIC BURDON

(handwritten: From Am to F#m)

Moderate beat

NC

(handwritten above staff: F#m)
Am

1. Hold your fire and lis-ten mis-ter.
2. There's one thing I got-ta say:____

Don't cause no trou-ble for my broth-er or sis-ter.
There's got-ta be some chang-es made.____

I HEARD IT THROUGH THE GRAPEVINE

Words and Music by
NORMAN WHITFIELD and BARRETT STRONG

3. People say believe half what you see
   Son, and none of what you hear;
   But I can't help bein' confused
   If it's true please tell me dear,
   Do you plan to let me go
   For the other guy you loved before?

IT'S A MAN'S WORLD

Words and Music b
JAMES BROWN and BETTY NEWSOM

Same

JOHNNY B GOODE

Words and Music by
CHUCK BERRY

MONSTER MASH

Words and Music by
BOBBY PICKETT and LEONARD CAPIZZI

Medium Rock Beat

Spoken: I was working in the lab late one night, when my eyes beheld

an eerie sight, for my monster from his slab began to rise, and

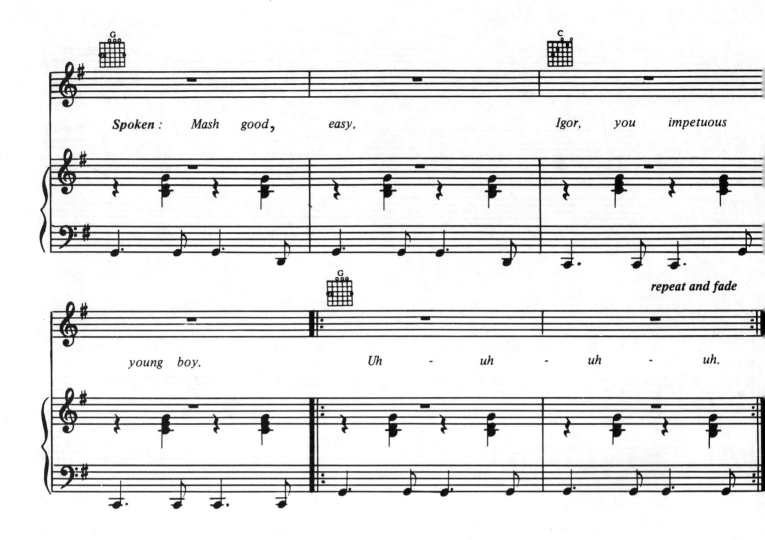

2. *From my laboratory in the castle east,*
   To the master bedroom where the vampires feast,
   The ghouls all came from their humble abodes
   To catch a jolt from my electrodes.
   (to Chorus: They did the mash)

3. *The zombies were having fun,*
   The party had just begun.
   The guests included Wolf-man,
   Dracula, and his son.

4. *The scene was rockin'; all were digging the sounds,*
   Igor on chains, backed by his baying hounds.
   The coffin - bangers were about to arrive
   With their vocal group "The Crypt- Kicker Five"
   (to Chorus: They played the mash)

5. *Out from his coffin, Drac's voice did ring;*
   Seems he was troubled by just one thing.
   He opened the lid and shook his fist,
   And said, "Whatever happened to my Translvanian twist?"
   (to Chorus: It's now the mash)

6. *Now everything's cool, Drac's a part of the band*
   And my monster mash is the hit of the land.
   For you, the living, this mash was meant too,
   *When you get to my door, tell them Boris sent you. **(till fade)***
   (to Chorus: And you can mash)

ROBOT MAN

Words and Music by
SYLVIA DEE and GEORGE GOEHRING

MR SPACEMAN

Words and Music by
JIM McGUINN

From G
To C

ONLY THE LONELY

Words and Music by
ROY ORBISON and JOE MELSON

ev - er _____ So far a - part _____ But ON - LY THE

LONE - LY _____ know_ why _____ I cry _____

ON - LY THE LONE - LY _____ ON - LY THE LONE - LY _____

- 2 -

ONLY THE LONELY know the heartaches I've been through
ONLY THE LONELY know I cry and cry for you
Maybe tomorrow, a new romance
No more sorrow, but that's the chance
You've got to take if you're lonely
Heartbreak, ONLY THE LONELY

SHE'S NOT THERE

Words and Music by
ROD ARGENT

A TEENAGER IN LOVE

Words and Music by
DOC POMUS and MORT SHUMAN

Each time we have a quar-rel it al-most breaks my heart,
One day I feel so hap-py; next day I feel so sad.

'Cause I am so a-'fraid that we will have to part.
I guess I'll learn to take the good ___ with the bad.

Each night I ask the stars up a-bove:

TELSTAR

By JOE MEEK

TELL HIM (TELL HER)

Words and Music by
BERT RUSSELL

WE'VE GOTTA GET OUT OF THIS PLACE

Words and Music by
BARRY MANN and CYNTHIA WEIL

Sing Optional 8va
You'll be dead be-fore your time is due I know
Watch my daddy in bed
C7
Eb7
Opt. 8va
— at night
Watch his hair been a turn-ing grey
He's been work-ing and sla-
Opt. 8va
-ving his life a-way
Oh yes I know it
I know he's been work-ing so hard
Opt. 8va
He's been work-ing so hard
I've — been work-ing too babe —

62

THE YOUNG ONES

Words and Music by
SID TEPPER and *ROY C. BENNETT*

Same

WHO'S SORRY NOW?

Words by BERT KALMAR and HARRY RUBY
Music by TED SNYDER

CHORUS

WIPEOUT

By WILSON, FULLER,
BERRYHILL and CONNOLLY

YOUNG GIRL

Words and Music by
JERRY FULLER

SHAKE RATTLE AND ROLL

From C
To E

Words and Music by
CHARLES CALHOUN

Moderately Bright

VERSE

Get out ___ from that kitch-en and rat-tle those pots and pans, ___

Get out ___ from that kitch-en and rat-tle those pots and pans. ___